A WORKABLE FAITH

A WORKABLE FAITH

JUNE SMALLWOOD WOOD

PHILOSOPHICAL LIBRARY
New York

Copyright, © 1974, by Philosophical Library, Inc.,

15 East 40th Street, New York, N. Y. 10016

All rights reserved

Library of Congress Catalog Card Number 74-80277

SBN 8022-2152-1

Printed in the United States of America

CONTENTS

Introduction	ix
Believe in God	11
The Parable of the Great Sculptor	21
The Fifth Dimension	23
Believe in Jesus	25
The Parable of the Three Travelers	35
The Eternal Brightness	41
Believe in the Holy Spirit	43
The Parable of the Wonderful Teacher	51
Living Wind	55
Enter the Kingdom of Heaven (or God)	57
The Parable of the Wise Lady	75
Immortal Legacy	77
Produce Spiritual Fruit	79
The Parable of the Oasis Garden	89
Seed of Heaven	93
Jesus and Prayer — June Wood—1962	95

A WORKABLE FAITH

INTRODUCTION

For the dozens of people I have met who want to have faith in Jesus, but who cannot find a faith that will satisfy their minds and work out in their living, I have written this book. It is my prayer that it will meet the need of this and other generations for a workable faith, and I believe it will, because it has worked for me.

BELIEVE IN GOD

Is there a God? is one of the oldest questions in history. Many brilliant and profound people have thought there is. King David, St. Paul, Voltaire, and Albert Einstein believed there is a God because of the natural law of the universe. David wrote:

The heavens declare the glory of God; and the firmament sheweth his handywork.

Day unto day uttereth speech, and night unto night showeth knowledge.

There is no speech nor language, where their voice is not heard. (Psalms 19: 1-3.)

Paul wrote in the first chapter of Romans, "Ever since the creation of the world his invisible nature, namely, his eternal power and deity, has been clearly perceived in the things that have been made."

Voltaire said, "The watch proves a watch-maker, and the Universe a God," and Einstein believed that the physical structure of the universe and its faithful natural laws proved divine mind. The thinking man may nod his head in agreement, but still wonder, "Does God have a personal interest in individual human beings?"

The very fact that man realizes there is divine mind back of the natural laws proves God cared enough to give man understanding. An unknown poet, writing about the wonders of music wrote:

> God is the author and not man; He laid
> The keynote of all harmonies; He planned
> All perfect combinations, and He made
> Us so that we could hear and understand.

Here then is the first and most obvious reason why a person should believe in God—the evidence of divine mind in nature and her laws, which man can observe and understand.

Even when the "Down Man" was crushing seeds with stone, he was also making crude religious symbols on the walls of his cave. Can it be that man is not just "incurably religious," but that the desire to worship (have contact) with a deity is as basic to his nature as his desire to have contact with other human beings—because he must? Do the first generation of birds hatched in the North, fly South because they know it will be warmer there during the winter, or because there is something in their natural makeup that compels them to start a flight across hundreds of uncharted miles? One psychologist kept birds in a synthetic setting, lighted with electricity and not the sun. When the rays of the artificial light were bent at the same angle as those of the spring sun's rays, the birds would become restless, and when released, fly North—even though it was winter. William James wrote, "Man is an animal who prays," and a thoughtful person will finish that statement with three words—*because he must!* Would there be this compulsion in the depths of man if there were not a "Being" who wanted to hear prayer? This basic need of man to pray is the second proof that there is not only a God, but one who is personally concerned with human beings.

Centuries before there was even an Old Testament, there were men who recognized the external proof of God, the creator in nature, and the internal proof of a God who was interested in man through their urges to pray. They began to make overtures to the "Creator and Prayer Giver," and found He was approachable. Their simple faith in this kind of God and His power to answer prayer is more courageous than the first journeys of men in boats upon the seas of the world; for they were experimenting with something that they would only feel the manifestations of, and they called that something spirit. Why does modern man choke upon the word spirit when, as far back as written history, it meant breath, air, or wind, and life? Who could live without breathing air? Spirit, then, is life itself, and therefore man called God spirit for He is that invisible force that moved them to pray and feel an answer. They called that part of themselves that felt His spirit moving them, their hearts and souls. Here then, is the second reason for believing in God, and that is that man can feel His Spirit working in their hearts and souls.

As these men observed the regeneration of life in the spring-time and the "survival of the fittest" in the animal world, they realized there was a "hereafter" or other world they could obtain if they lived the way that pleased God: only what kind of a God did they worship and what pleased Him?

There were many different ideas about the type of spiritual being God was, or the personality that He had; and so, there appeared among the tribes of men, different religions about the same God. Most of these religions fell into corruption because men could not worship a God of both good and evil; and so the majority of men feared suffering and felt that God caused it, and their lives were lived in fear as they tried through all kinds of cults to appease God's wrath. A few thinking people felt that the elements of fear and evil which brought suffering to men were caused by a lesser spiritual being who was not worthy to be worshipped. This spiritual being was later called Satan, the Devil, The Serpent or Dragon, or The Prince of Darkness (or of This World) in the Bible. There were only a few men who really believed God was kind and wanted men to act in kind ways instead of low and brutish animal ways. Only a few of these were ever able to control themselves enough to try out in their lives what they believed. Here then is another reason for believing in God. He is kind and expects men to be, also. The proof of this is that a few men have been kind, too.

Soon men began to keep a record of the men who believed and lived like this; and so the Old Testament came into being. It could easily be called a History of Spiritual Giants. Modern man usually believes that there is one God, creator of the universe, who is kind and cares for people in some vague way, but they balk at the idea of believing in the Bible as the best guide man has for knowing God's will, that tells what conduct pleases God in the lives of men. Communists look upon the Bible as a book of superstition, because they do not think it agrees with the scientific idea of creation. The Bible was written by people who had never heard of the word science, but it does not conflict in general principle with scientific ideas. The acts of creation are the same as the Geological ages. Even the mist which went up from the earth and watered the whole face of the ground (Gen. 2:6), is recorded in Geological history, and all scientists agree that only life begets life. That Adam and Eve were the first couple on the earth is not the question, because there is a complete account of the creation of the heavens and the earth and finally "man" who was called "them," in the first chapter of Genesis.

In the second chapter of Genesis there is another story about "the man" whom God formed out of the dust of the ground and breathed into his nostrils the breath of life; and "he" became a living soul. This "the man," and there is a definite article before this "man" called he, not them, was not put on earth to have dominion over it and all the wild animals, but in a garden where he was to keep all the beautiful and edible vegetation for the Lord, and enjoy the Lord's company. This man who was a living soul was called Adam, and according to the *Interpreter's Bible Dictionary,* Adam was a proper name for one individual in this second chapter, and though the exact meaning of this name is not known, the nearest any of the scholars can come to it is the phrase, "to be red." A little more study on the part of the Bible student will reveal to him that Adam was probably not the first man, because his son Cain married a woman in Nod, who was not his sister, but that the man, Adam, was the first living soul or human being with whom God had any close communion.

This extremely literal interpretation of the creation of man and "the man," Adam, would explain the difference in the time element in the Bible story of man, and the Geological story of man's beginnings. At the same time it would remove the shadow of mythology that figurative interpretations have hung over the following chapters. When the unbeliever declares that there is mythology in the Bible and points out that in the sixth chapter of Genesis that the sons of God came into the daughters of man and soon there were giants on the earth, the believer can remind him that this is merely an explanation of the union of Adam's sons and the daughters of other men created earlier, because St. Luke wrote in the third chapter of his gospel, "Adam, which was the son of God. . . ."

These peculiar unions produced giants or Nephilim, men of renown, according to the Bible story. This is probably a very real fact, because the *Encyclopaedia Britannica* states that there were two types of men in existence during these early times, and they were the Neanderthal man, low and brutish, and the Cro-Magnon man whose average height, at a time when the average man was very low, was six feet or better on the average, and this man's skull was at least an inch or two larger than that of the Neanderthal. There actually were giants on the earth, because their bones have been found as far South as Palestine, and as far North as southern France. As for the great flood, no people have ever lived whose ancient history does not tell of a universal flood, from which only one family survived. If, however this strains the faith of a believer, he will be relieved to find that geologists are finding large pillows of salt buried deep in the ground in the place where this large local flood probably happened.

It is even interesting to note that Chaldea and Egypt, the places where metals were first used (5,000 B.C.) were also the places where Noah, Abraham, and Moses lived. Could not the same places that produced men of superior knowledge about tools also produce men with superior knowledge about God, and what pleased Him.

The great men of the Bible did not have their lives recorded in the book of books because they made highly exciting reading (some of them did) but because they discovered things or rather truths about God and His spiritual laws that worked in the lives of men. Here is where more people lose their faith than any other way, and that is they think or have been led to believe that every word in the Bible is the word of God. This is an unworkable belief, and is not true, because most of the Old Testament is history, telling how these men discovered the spiritual truths, and very often these men made mistakes before and after they discovered or had truths revealed to them.

When God speaks directly to man through the Bible, it is stated so. There is no doubt that the Ten Commandments came direct from God to man, but the hundreds of lesser laws that are in the Old Testament that could only work for a nomadic tribe of Jews in the wilderness, came from the necessity of the times, and were probably given by Moses, and his followers when the need for them arose. There is always one yardstick to measure Scripture by to see if it originated straight from God or from the history being recorded to explain man's progress in his knowledge of Godliness, and that is does it work out in a life of love. Men do not use the Ten Commandments because they are in the Bible, but men use the Ten Commandments—even as a basis for *all* law—because they work out in a life of love just like 2+2 always makes 4 in a mathematical problem. Long before the word pragmatic or workable was ever heard of, men were using the spiritual laws from God for their own moral and spiritual well-being. Here then is another reason for believing in God—his truths, as recorded in the Bible, are workable. He is both kind and just.

When a person reads the Bible seeking spiritual truths that are direct from God to man and not part of the Bible story, he should know that for the devout and scholarly Jew, and especially the rabbis of Jesus' day, there were four different ways to interpret Scripture, and some passages might easily be interpreted in two or maybe even more of these ways. Dr. William Barclay in his book *Letters to the Galatians and Ephesians,* gives these four methods of interpretation. They are 1) Peshat, which is the simple or literal meaning; 2) Remaz, which is the suggested meaning; 3) Derush, which is the evolved and deduced meaning, and 4) Sod, which is the allegorical meaning.

No matter which way a person interprets the whole Bible, certain spiritual truths and ideas are there and remain the same for all men whether they have a literal or figurative interpretation of the Bible, and they are:

I.—God, the supreme spiritual being, creator of the Universe, approachable, kind and just, and interested and lovingly concerned with man.

II.—Man, the climax of God's earthly creation, designed by his maker to commune with and obey God.

III.—Satan, a lesser spiritual being or corrupt angel, representing Evil or darkness, called The Serpent, unworthy of man's obedience, yet enticing man to disobey God.

IV.—Man, suffering because he has disobeyed God and has become vulnerable to the oppression (sin, sickness and death), many of which are undeserved, of Satan.

V.—God, giving man divine help through prayer, the law, and the prophets, in his battle with Satan, and even choosing a race to express to the world these spiritual truths, which finally brings forth a God-man, Jesus who fully expresses and explains God's desires and designs for man.

Without Jesus, God would still be worth worshipping, but he would be merely a benevolent despot. But with Jesus all the benevolence of God is expressed in Fatherly love, and all the laws, truths and prophets are suddenly heightened to this love for one's children, not one's subjects. What a difference this makes in a person's worship, when he knows the Father of Jesus.

Boris Pasternak, in his book *Doctor Zhivago,* writes about how dark and cruel the world was under Roman rule, "And then *He came,*" and all things changed. The first thing in creation was light, and Jesus said, "I am the light of the world," and He really is. No other religion in the world has a Messiah who is "the way, the truth, and the life." The way of life to please God is the way Jesus lived it. The truth about spiritual things are the words of Jesus, and the life eternal is the life which Jesus laid down as a sacrifice to redeem men out of the clutches of Satan. Here then, is the crowning reason to believe and worship God—namely his perfect grace or loving kindness. What loving parent would give his son to die for the sins of his neighbor's children? It is almost impossible for humans to believe that God would do this, much less, understand why. Who is worthy of such love? No one!

Can it be that God is so absolutely loving and merciful, that He did this for worthless humanity? God's gracious character, and not man's worthiness is the only reason for the life, death, and resurrection of Jesus. That such a man lived is proof there is not only One, kind, just, approachable, creator God, but God so infinitely loving that man can only guess as to what He has prepared for those who worship Him.

THE PARABLE OF THE GREAT SCULPTOR

There was once a wise man and a smart fool who came to a studio of a great sculptor, and unaware of where they were, they went in. All about them in the main room were the first works of the great master. These first works were very crude; for they were merely small round casts of plaster that he had used to learn how to make a perfect cell. Then there were small chains of these cells done in clay, and at last many strange and complicated designs done in marble, but still made up of the small cells. Huge statues of unknown birds, giant beasts, and finally men, filled his inner studio, and both the wise man and the fool stood in wonder as they looked at the great variety of works. As they were doing this, the great sculptor was hiding behind the heavy curtains that led into his glorious garden from the inner studio, waiting to see what they would say and do about his art.

The wise man was at once humbled and cried out, "Look at these wonderful things that someone made. The artist must be a genius. Let us worship him!"

The smart fool was horrified, and looked at the wise man and shook his head as he said, "How can you say such a thing! Why these things are bound to be some kind of freak accident, because they are not of the same age, they are made of different substances, and no one could conceive of so many different and varied things."

The wise man smiled kindly and replied, "Friend, they may be of different ages, but they are all of the same cell unit. Even if their substance is different, they gradually progress in complexity through their stages, and that proves the planning and creative power of divine mind."

The smart fool looked at his companion in scorn and said, "You are not as smart as I, and you would teach me? There is nothing here but chaos, which is what my life is really—just chaos and the struggle to live. I will never be as stupid as you." The smart fool left the studio, and went and told others about the accident he had found. Many more smart fools came to the studio and agreed with him. The wise man stayed longer and examined the pieces of art more carefully, and became more and more convinced that they were created by divine mind. He, then, went and told the world of his discovery and its importance, and many came to the studio and believed him.

When the great sculptor realized that the wise man really understood his art and had convinced others about the way it was made and who had made it, he drew aside the heavy curtain, and called to the wise man, "Come with me to Paradise, where greater things than you have ever dreamed of are waiting for us to see together."

THE FIFTH DIMENSION

There is a Fifth Dimension in our lives
That transcends height and depth and breadth and time
And it is faith, that feels there is a Mind Divine,
And calls it God, a name as old as man himself.
Some say, He is impersonal and far removed,
Dedicated to the rigid law. I say He cares
More than a mortal mind will ever know,
Because we know the Giver and the Law.
He made us so. He even broke through time
With such a force of Love sublime,
We stand in wonder at the Cross,
Amazed that He who put the stars against the dark,
Would stoop to lift us mortals to His heart.

BELIEVE IN JESUS

Many people have believed that Jesus was born in Bethlehem, lived most of His life about Galilee, and died on a cross outside of Jerusalem. Many people have thought He was a spiritual genius, just as Alexander the Great was a military genius. Many, many small and great religions have Jesus as a prophet or spiritual leader as part of their creed. (The Jewish and Islamic religions being only two of these.) There are, however, even in so-called Christian countries, only a few people who really believe that Jesus is the Son of God.

This is not surprising, because James, His own brother, did not believe this until after Jesus' resurrection. If His own brother doubted, why should anyone believe that Jesus is the Son of God? There are many reasons for believing Jesus is the Son of God, but none as strong as the fact that He was expected. No other religion has a Messiah whose appearance on earth was anticipated for literally hundreds of years. Even as early as the first chapter of Genesis, the Bible reader finds allusions to spiritual sons of God.

To whom was God speaking when He said, "Let us make man in our image, after our likeness, (Genesis 1: 26) and "Behold, the man has become like one of us, (Genesis 3: 22)? Other spiritual beings! Could it be that God was referring to the Jewish people and ultimately Jesus, their gift to the world, when He told the serpent, or Satan:

> "I will put enmity between you and the woman,
> And between your seed and her seed;
> He shall bruise your head,
> And you shall bruise His heel." (Gen. 3: 15.)

To whom was He speaking when He saw the tower of Babel and said, "Come, let us go down and there confuse their language." His heavenly sons! God told Abraham that "Abraham shall become a great and mighty nation and all the nations of the earth shall bless themselves by him." (Gen. 18: 18) and He also made this promise to Jacob. (Gen. 28: 14.)

Jacob promised his grandson Judah, "The sceptre shall not depart from Judah, nor a law giver from between his feet until Shiloh come; and unto him shall the gathering of the people be. (Gen. 49: 10.) Webster says that the word Shiloh is Hebrew for the name given the Messiah by Jacob.

In the Septuagint, the Bible of the Alexandrian Jews, there is a very clear-cut, vivid prediction of the virgin birth of the Messiah, and King David, who always referred to himself as "I" or "me," wrote the 110th Psalm, which begins, "The Lord said to my Lord: sit at my right hand, till I make your enemies your footstool." Isaiah foretells in the 53d chapter of Isaiah, of a person who is called "he," while the people to whom Isaiah is writing is called "we," who, "makes himself an offering for sin." This whole chapter so perfectly describes the life, death, and eternal kingship of Jesus that it leaves no doubt in the mind of the reader that Jesus was the long-expected Messiah, Holy One of Israel, or Emmanuel, about whom all the Scripture and the prophets foretold. Jesus himself said, "before Abraham was; I am." (John 8: 50.) No other religious leader—be he Socrates, Buddha, Confucius, Lao-tze, Mohammed or anyone else was ever able to declare that God had pre-announced his earthly parents; his birthplace; his character, acts and personality; his death—even as to whom he would die with, and finally his eternal kingship. The fact that Jesus fulfilled all prophecy is His proof that He is the Son of God.

A second reason for believing Jesus is the Son of God is that He gave new meaning to many truths, some of which were adapted from the Old Testament, by actually living them out in His own life. He proved truth by demonstrating it. Other religious writers before and after Christ, and many Old Testament writers and prophets have stated many of the truths He taught, but no other person ever combined them into one ministry, and then lived all of them out in one lifetime—even a lifetime of thirty three years. The reason Jesus could give the great commission—go teach, go preach, go heal, was, because He had not only taught these things, but had done them in His own life. Buddha gave sound advice and peace to his followers, but his hands were never outstretched in forgiveness and healing. Mohammed wrote many fine truths that sound like the best of the Old Testament, and at times as lofty as some of the teachings of Jesus, but he had many wives, engaged in holy wars, did not live a life of non-violence, and finally ruled an earthly kingdom. A truly honest person can make a thorough study of all the religions, but He can not find one religious teacher or prophet who lived out such high moral teachings.

Christ proved His divinity at His crucifixion when He forgave His executioners, and so impressed the hardened Roman centurion that he said, "Truly, this was the Son of God." (Matt. 27: 54.)

Another important reason for believing Jesus is the Son of God is, He performed miracles that have never been equaled either in quantity or quality. It is almost impossible for the scientific mind of this century to realize these miracles really happened, but there were no wonder drugs that could suddenly heal the sick in the time of Jesus. Miracles were common, however, but most of these miracles were nothing more than magic, very similar to those a magician on a modern stage would perform. According to the Interpreter's Bible, there were whole cults and books to enlighten anyone who wanted to practice this type of magical miracles that flourished in the Grecian-Roman culture of Jesus' day. The Book of Acts tells of several times when the apostles met magicians. The story throwing the most insight on this idea of miracles is found in the Eighth Chapter of Acts and tells of Simon the magician who had amazed Samaria with his magic, and who offered John and Peter money to give him the secret of the laying on of hands to receive the Holy Spirit.

There was also the practice of Black Magic or witchcraft, but most of these miracles were hideous deeds of poisoning or the use of harmful drugs for the purpose of sorcery.

The other type of miracle that was most common in the time of Jesus was the casting out of devils, considered by most experts today as the type of disorder that only modern Psychiatry could heal, as they were of an emotional origin. Since most doctors think that at least fifty percent of all disorders even in the most stable people are of this nature, it is very likely that in a land where the main drugs were wine, myrrh, and oil for wounds, this was the only cure for every disorder, and if it was not emotional in nature then there was no cure.

Jesus was very careful to explain to the Pharisees that He was performing the same miracles as their sons with "the finger of God . . ." (Luke 11: 19-20) when he cast out devils. He did not work any magic, but He performed many acts of casting out evil spirits or devils which was a fairly common practice for His day, but most important, he performed miracles which have never been equaled before or since—the healing of the man born blind from birth, and the healing of the Gadarene demoniac are but two examples of disorders of this type.

The Jews of Jesus' day were expecting a Messiah who would perform signs similar to those of Moses and Elijah, who both had the power to part the waters of seas and rivers. It was this kind of miracle that the scribes and Pharisees wanted to see when they demanded a "Sign" of Jesus, who answered, "An evil and adulterous generation seeketh after a sign; and there shall no sign be given to it, but the sign of the prophet Jonah." (Matt. 12: 39.)

Dr. Frederick Grant in his book, *New Testament Thought*, writes, "The evidence for the greatest miracle of all, Jesus' resurrection, is stated repeatedly by Paul (I Cor. 15: 3-18, probably the first written account), by John (Chs. 20-21), by Mark (16: 16), by Luke (Ch. 24) and by Matthew (27: 62-68: 28.) And though this testimony is difficult to harmonize, a fact quite in keeping with its diversity (if one man had invented the story, the whole body of evidence would be easily harmonized and self-consistent). The amplitude and importance of it for the early church is not to be questioned."

That Jesus was really dead was proved for certain when the soldier pierced His side, and the blood and water came out—a certain sign of death. The character of the people who saw His death and resurrection is another very strong reason for believing this fact, (He even ate food before them, and let them feel of His hands and side) but the behavior of the disciples following Pentecost is the strongest proof of Jesus' resurrection. No one will give his entire life with enthusiasm even unto death for a hoax. Here then is the third and most ignored proof of Jesus' divinity—His miracles that were stamped with God's approval in His resurrection.

A fourth reason for believing Jesus is the Son of God, is His impact upon history. There are dozens of men who made remarkable contributions in deeds, or writings, or discoveries, and one would say they made their dent or scratch on history, but Jesus struck history with such an impact that in the Western world all time before His birth is called B.C. and all time after His birth is called A.D. This slightly educated son of a Galilean carpenter or handyman wrote nothing but a few words in the sand; yet, this itinerant preacher struck history with such an impact that He changed the religious and social ideas of the world for all time.

The first change was that the need for all animal sacrifice ceased! In the fourth chapter of Genesis, the reader finds that "Able brought of the firstlings of his flock," as an offering and it pleased God. From then on, a sacrifice of a spotless lamb was considered the highest form of worship. When the Hebrew people were slaves in Egypt they killed lambs and smeared their blood on their houses; so that the death angel would pass over their homes; and from then on, the Pascal Lamb was considered the supreme atonement. When John the Baptist saw Jesus coming toward him, he said, "Behold the Lamb of God, who takes away the sin of the world!" (John 1: 29.) Jesus said, "For this reason the Father loves Me, because I lay down My life that I may take it again. No other takes it from me, but I lay it down of my own accord. I have power to lay it down and I have power to take it again; this charge have I received from My Father." (John 10: 17, 18.) Jesus was God's perfect or spotless lamb. Perhaps He was a volunteer. Many of Jesus' remarks cause the reader to think He volunteered for the place of the atoning sacrifice, and His death upon the cross was so completely sufficient, that wherever the Gospel is preached and understood, ritual sacrifice ceases. No one should feel pangs of guilt for any sin when Jesus shed His blood to erase all sin.

Jesus said to the woman at the well at Samaris, "Woman,

believe Me, the hour is coming when neither on this mountain, nor in Jerusalem will you worship the Father. . . . But the hour is coming, and now is when the true worshipers will worship the Father in spirit and truth, for such the Father seeks to worship Him. God is spirit, and those who worship Him must worship in spirit and truth." (John 4: 21, 23, 24.) In this statement Jesus revealed things about God that caused two religious ideas to change.

The first was that of a Jewish God who could be worshipped best in Jerusalem, and the second was that of a spiritual being who was so far off that only with great ritual and sacrifice could a few very devout, law-abiding Jews ever make contact with him. Jesus gave to the world a Universal God of spirit and truth, and now there are churches or temples on most of the corners of the world. The average Christian feels that all these buildings are not sufficient to hold God's spirit.

Jesus also gave to the world a God so very gracious and loving that Jesus called Him Father, and declared to the world that He was interested even in children, lepers and sinners. This idea of God the Father of all mankind caused and is still causing great social reforms. Three of the most noticeable are the emancipation of women, the care and interest of the world in little children, and the equalizing of all men politically. Bishop Fulton J. Sheen in his remarkable book, *Go to Heaven,* wrote, "Since a fallen angel tempted the first woman to rebel, God now consults through an unfallen angel, Gabriel, with the new Eve, Mary, and asks, "Will you give me a man? . . . When this plan was presented to Mary in the greatest charter of freedom the world ever heard, she answered, "Be it done unto me according to Thy Word." This man, Jesus, that was conceived in her by the Holy Spirit, treated the women in His life with more love and respect than any man who has ever lived.

He forgave the adulteress, even healed the Syro-Phenician woman's daughter, and first appeared after His resurrection to Mary Magdalene! Wherever His life has been read and understood by men, polygamy has ceased and women have been treated with consideration and love.

At the same time and almost in the same way, He turned the love and attention of the world on little children. He raised the ruler's daughter from the dead, blessed the little children declaring that people who were childlike were greatest in the Kingdom of Heaven, and even went so far as to tell the rulers in the temple on Palm Sunday that, "Out of the mouths of babes and sucklings, 'God has brought perfect praise!'" (Matthew 21: 16.)

His idea that made the greatest impact upon history was "that *everyone* who sees the Son and believes in Him should have eternal life; and I will raise him up at the last day." (John 6: 40.) If Jesus openly offered eternal life to *everyone*, who is man to deny any earthly right to anyone? Wherever His words have been preached and believed, the artificial stratas of society are surely breaking down. Only the Son of God could have made such an impact upon history.

The greatest reason for believing that Jesus is the Son of God is the impact He had and still has on individual lives. He changed the twelve quarreling disciples into saintly men. He struck down Saul of Tarsus, and turned him into St. Paul, the greatest missionary of all time. He took the life of the lustful Augustine and so completely changed it that he became the gentle Bishop of Hippo. The sight of a dead tree, reminded a coarse Seventeenth-century footsoldier named Nicholas Herman of the death and resurrection of Jesus and on the spot he received Christ as his savior and experienced such a spiritual change that his name became Brother Lawrence and he wrote the Christian classic, *The Practice of the Presence of God.*

The power or impact of Jesus on human lives is most vividly seen in the life of John Bunyan, who had only a few years of formal education. When he was put in prison for preaching the Gospel, he taught himself to read and write fluently, and then made shoestrings and earned enough money to secure pencil and paper and write *Pilgrim's Progress,* one of the masterpieces of Christian literature and also the greatest allegory in all English literature.

Frank Laubach, the twentieth-century Christian leader and world educator, wrote in his spiritual diary, *Learning the Vocabulary of God,* "This attempt to keep my will bent toward Your (Jesus) will is integrating me." Ah, yes, the greatest proof that Jesus is the Son of God is His impact upon the lives of people today.

He meets the needs of the individual of every age. It is possible for a person to live without being loved, but it is not possible for a person to "live" in any sense of the word "live" without loving. Jesus is the perfect love object for any man or woman. Who can read His life without falling in love with Him? And He answers all love. There is no unrequited love with Jesus! Who can follow only a few of Jesus' instructions, even in the feeblest way, without finding meaning and direction in his life? No one! Who can read about Jesus' victories over all the oppressions of Satan, (sin, sickness, and even death) without feeling great surges of character and strength for victorious living? Yes, Jesus answers the need of individuals for love, purpose, and courage! This is why He still makes such an impact on individual lives today.

If anyone doubts this, let him read the life of Christ as recorded in the Gospels and ask this same Jesus who is the same yesterday, today, and forever, to make him a disciple.

If the person is really sincere, Jesus will certainly use him, and change him wonderfully, even as He changed all those mentioned here. Then the new Christian will cry, "Jesus is the Son of God."

THE PARABLE OF THE THREE TRAVELERS

There were once three travelers on the road of life. As they began their journey, they were gay and carefree friends. The first traveler told his companions that he longed to gain wealth, fame, and the approval of men. The second traveler told his companions that he wanted to be happy, contented, and get along with everybody. The third traveler pointed to a high mountain in the far distance and told his companions that he wanted to climb that mountain so he could look down upon everything and everyone and understand the reason for their journey. His friends laughed at him, because the mountain was very high, and there was no path that could be seen leading to the top. Soon the travelers began to grow weary of each other's company, because they were not looking for the same gate to turn into to gain their ends.

It was not long before the first traveler saw a gate of gold that was bright and beautiful, and he began to try to enter. His companions watched him as he beat upon the gate. It was not long before a handsome sentry opened the gate to him, and asked him what he wanted. The first traveler replied, "I want to go the way of the Golden Gate."

The sentry replied, "Are you willing to pay the price? Those who go the way of the Golden Gate must leave their souls outside, because it is a way that demands soulless living."

"I am glad to leave my soul outside," cried the first traveler, and shook off his soul like a dog shakes off fleas and entered the way of the Golden Gate.

Immediately, he was surrounded by gay, well-dressed friends who were eager to help him enjoy his wealth and elect him to some office that he was seeking. They dressed him in a fine uniform and followed him about to the beat of drums that were in a band. There was a parade. Soon, however, he found that he must lead his army of friends against other people who were very much like himself and his friends, only they were wearing different uniforms. His side was victorious, and those of his new friends who had not been killed in the little war he had caused, were crying out for more wars, and more parades, and more fun. He tried again, and this time the shouts of his followers sounded more like jeers. He listened closely to hear which of his so-called friends betrayed him, and when the battle was over, he had them put to death. Soon, there was so much friction and strife among the group that he led that they lost their next battle, and he was led away captive to another man in a different uniform who pushed him out into the darkness that surrounded the road he had chosen. Here he lamented his fate. His uniform was soiled and the brass and braid was tarnished and heavy. He was utterly lost and called out for someone to help him, but his once gay companions were either as lost as he was or had followed a new leader into a new adventure.

He wept bitterly and cried out again for help, but his voice became weaker and weaker, and no one answered. At last, in desperation, he began to run about wildly, hoping to find the light and his gay friends again, but in the darkness he became confused and fell into a deep abyss and died.

The two other travelers, quite unaware of what had happened to the first, went on down the road of life, seeking the gates that would lead them to their destination. Very soon, they came to the broad gate of Contentment. The second traveler thought this was just what he was looking for, and knocked at the gate. A pleasant committee of congenial people looked out, and asked him what he wanted. "I want to enter the broad gate of Contentment," said the second traveler.

The committee replied, "Are you willing to pay the price? Those who go the way of the broad gate of Contentment must put on the cloak of indifference forever."

"I am glad to put on the cloak of indifference," cried the second traveler, and the committee brought out the cloak and he wrapped it securely about him.

At once, he found himself inside the gate and surrounded by pleasant and congenial friends who were having an eternal good time. One day they would play cards; the next day they would go boating or pleasure driving; and the next day they would have a huge party. Occasionally, they would form a hobby club, and there each person would follow the hobby that most interested him. This went on for days and weeks and months, and finally years. The second traveler became very unhappy, because everyone was so completely indifferent to each other's needs. If there was anyone who was in any way different or who needed help, the group just pushed him aside. At last the second traveler became sick to death of doing nothing but just what the group wanted forever, and he cried out for help. The group was utterly indifferent to him, just as they had been to all the other travelers who were not doing like the group.

Finally, the poor traveler lay down to die. "Will no one help me now?" he begged, but the group said, "How can we? We must always wear the cloak of indifference, and you did not help anyone; so why should we help you."

The second traveler lay down beside the gay company and rolled over so he could not see them dancing beside him, and there he died.

The third traveler went on alone, because he did not want to give up his soul or wear the cloak of indifference. Finally he saw a very narrow gate to the side of the road. He went to the gate and knocked. There was a man standing there with a crown of thorns pressed down upon his brow, who said, "Friend, what brings you to the gate of the Cross?"

The third traveler said, "I could not give up my soul or wear the cloak of indifference, but I long to climb the mountain to see what this journey is all about."

"This is the gate that leads to the top of the mountain, and many have entered here, but few have ever succeeded. You must be willing to follow me; for I am the way, the truth, and the life. No man can reach the mountaintop without following me."

"I will follow you wherever you lead me, master; only let me in the gate of the Cross," cried the traveler.

The man opened the gate and the third traveler squeezed through. "Before we can go any farther," said the man, "You must surrender everything to me—your thoughts, your feelings, and your belongings. This is the first test on the way of the Cross."

"I surrender all to you master," cried the third traveler.

"Follow me. I am the light of the world, and wherever you see light, that is the path you are to follow. Look down, and you will see drops of blood, which mark the way of the Cross."

The first part of the journey was glorious, because the light from the man made the way easy, but it was not long before they were in a wilderness. The man turned to the traveler and said, "We are in the wilderness of temptation, and almost all souls are lost here because they do not know how to resist the tempter here. If you know the Word, you will pass, but if you do not you will die here," and the man gave the traveler a book to read.

The traveler read the book carefully, and as soon as he had, the tempter approached him. First, he tempted the traveler with food for his body, but he refused. Next he tempted him with glamorous talents that would startle the whole world, but the traveler refused to follow him. Finally, the tempter offered the traveler the kingship of the whole earth, but the traveler knew that this was only a trick, and so he refused even this temptation, because he knew the Word.

"You have done well," said the man, but "Can you follow me into the valley of hard work and human suffering?" and he led the traveler into the valley where hundreds of hungry, sick, dirty, and wicked people clawed at them for help. The traveler did not draw back from their ugliness and needs, but helped the man as he ministered to each of them.

They began to climb higher and the air grew thinner and the way steeper and the man turned to the traveler and said, "You have done well to follow me this far, but can you believe in miracles?" and he called forth the dead prophets and the patriarchs and they conversed together. "I believe," said the traveler, and once again they climbed the mountain together.

As they climbed higher, throngs of people followed them, until at last, they were on a narrow ledge with a large crowd crying after them. The man turned to the traveler and said, "Can you follow me along the narrow ledge of vain glory? The crowd that you see following us, wants to make us earthly rulers, because we have satisfied their needs. Can you stay on the ledge of vain glory and not become tempted away by the good opinions of men?"

The traveler nodded and kept his eyes on the man and followed him along the narrow ledge of vain glory.

Suddenly, they were in a lonely garden and it was night and strangely cold. "Where are we now, master?" asked the traveler. "In the garden of Gethsemane," replied the man. "Here you may turn back, because here you must decide to face ridicule and shame and even death for me—even the death of the Cross," but the traveler went ahead with the man.

The air grew colder and the darkness thickened, and the traveler cried out in pain as he struggled to breathe, "Master, where are we?"

And the man replied, "We are at the Cross. Do not be disheartened. It is almost over."

There was utter stillness and complete darkness, and the traveler saw or felt nothing until he heard the voice of the man calling him, and he answered, "Master, where are we now?"

"Look down," was the answer. "Look down, weary traveler. You have succeeded. You are at the top of the mountain with me."

THE ETERNAL BRIGHTNESS

Eternal Brightness of the Universe, conceived before the sun was made,
Shine Spirit rays upon our mortal clay.
Eternal Brightness from whose fire the stars were set ablaze,
Spark our cold souls and kindle warm and loving fires.
Let your white heat consume all darkness of the night,
Illumine all the crevices of fear that we must face;
For your pure light can change the darkest stain to brightest white.
Cleanse all our hearts, and burn in good and kind desires.
Eternal Brightness, shine and glow and gleam more bright;
For we, like cold dead moons before the suns,
Will ever be in darkness till your light
Glows on our mortal clay and makes it shine—
Reflecting to the earth below, Thy light divine.

BELIEVE IN THE HOLY SPIRIT

Jesus told Nicodemus, "The wind blows where it wills and you hear the sound of it, but you do not know whence it comes or whither it goes; so it is with every one who is born of the Spirit." (John 3: 8.) Just before the great flood when man's wickedness had become unbearable to God, He said, "My spirit shall not abide in man forever, for he is flesh." (Genesis 6: 3.) Jesus told His disciples in the synagogue in Capernaum, "It is the spirit that gives life; the flesh is of no avail; the words that I have spoken to you are spirit and life." (John 6: 63.) If all these statements are true then God's spirit was breathed out into the world through the words of Jesus and this was accomplished by the Holy Spirit.

According to the Hastings Bible Dictionary, the idea of the Holy Spirit as the Christian today knows it, or is supposed to know it, was not clear until New Testament times. Jesus clearly tells his disciples the facts about the Holy Spirit at the Last Supper. He said, "If you love me, you will keep my commandments. And I will pray to the Father, and he will give you another Counselor, to be with you forever, even the Spirit of truth, whom the world cannot receive, because it neither sees him nor knows him; you know him, for he dwells with you, and will be in you. (John 14; 15; 17.) Then He also told them. "But the Counselor, the Holy Spirit, whom the Father will send in My name, He will teach you all things, and bring to your remembrance all that I have said to you." (John 14: 26.) These promises and the fact that Jesus declared the Spirit a teacher as well as using the pronoun "He," makes the Holy Spirit the third person of the Godhead, and at the same time God's invisible but active force to carry out His will from the beginning of time until the very end. The main purpose of the Holy Spirit or His greatest work is to move the affections of human beings toward God.

This idea of the work and person of the Holy Spirit was not clear at all during Old Testament times. The writers of these books knew that some force was coming into their lives from God, and they called it spirit. The word spirit in the Bible literally means wind, air or breath. In the very first chapter, the first verse of Genesis is written, "and the Spirit (or wind) of God moved upon the face of the water," and in the second chapter of Genesis is written ". . . then the Lord God formed man of dust from the ground and breathed into his nostrils the breath of life, and man became a living soul."

In fact, the words Holy Spirit only appear three times (Isaiah 63: 10 & 11, and Psalms 51: 11) in the Old Testament and even then only the word Spirit is capitalized. The phrase "In the spirit," "inspired by the spirit" and King David's own words, "The spirit of the Lord speaks by me, His word is upon my tongue," clearly show that the patriarchs, kings and prophets felt that when they wrote or spoke what later became the very words of God apart from the Bible Story, that God Himself was speaking to them. These visitations were always to only a few people of great character and spiritual insight, and their inspired writings were often called the Word (of God); therefore the Word and the Spirit were almost interchangeable. In fact, the Gospel of John begins, "In the beginning was the Word, and the Word was with God, and the Word was God. He was in the beginning with God. . . ." (John 1: 1-2.) Here then is the first reason for believing in the Holy Spirit and that is, even though He was not well understood, He is mentioned in the Old Testament, even the first chapter of Genesis; and also under His influence was all inspired Scripture written.

The capitalized words Holy Spirit first appear in the New Testament in the first chapter of Luke. The angel that appeared to Zachariah foretold that John the Baptist "will be filled with the Holy Spirit, even from his Mother's womb." This same angel, Gabriel, told Mary, "The Holy Spirit will come upon you," and this visitation caused the child that was born to her, even though she was a virgin, to be the "Son of God." This same Holy Spirit temporarily filled Elizabeth when she saw Mary, and revealed to Elizabeth that Mary was to be the Mother of Jesus. Again this same temporal visitation occurred to Zachariah when he prophesied after naming his son, John. And this same experience occurred to Simeon when he saw the Baby Jesus in the temple in Jerusalem and knew He was the Christ.

When John was preaching in the wilderness, he declared that he had been told (by God, undoubtedly) that the one on whom the Holy Spirit descended and remained would be the one who would baptize with the Holy Spirit. This, of course, was Jesus, whose baptism with water and with the Holy Spirit were almost simultaneous. Here, then, is another reason for believing in the Holy Spirit, and that is many people, including Jesus and John, experienced the Holy Spirit, and this was before the time of Pentecost.

Until the time of Jesus, no person had ever been "full" of the Holy Spirit and in the power of the Spirit. His disciples knew he had exceedingly wonderful spiritual gifts, but they could not understand from where this power came and exactly what it was. When one disciple asked Jesus to teach them to pray, Jesus first gave them the Lord's prayer and then said, "Ask and it will be given you—If you then, who are evil, know how to give good gifts to your children, how much more will the Heavenly Father give the Holy Spirit to those who ask Him?" (Luke 11: 9, 13.) When the mother of James and John asked that her sons should sit on the right and left of Jesus in His kingdom, Jesus answered, "Are you able . . . to be baptized with the baptism with which I am baptized?" (Mark 10: 38.) After Jesus' resurrection and just before His ascension, He told His disciples not to leave Jerusalem, "for John baptized with water, but before many days you shall be baptized with the Holy Spirit." (Acts 1: 5.) This is the third reason for believing in the Holy Spirit, and that is that Jesus instructed His followers to both ask for and experience the Holy Spirit.

It is interesting to most Christians that the Holy Spirit took the bodily form of a dove, when Jesus was baptized. The dove was, of course, the bird that Noah sent out of the Ark, and it brought back the olive branch. Two doves were also the sacrifice of purification for poor people, and so the choice of a dove as the symbol of the Holy Spirit shows that God means for this baptism to bring meekness, cleanliness, and peace to a person humble enough to accept his baptism. Here is the fourth reason why a person should believe in the Holy Spirit, and that is that only the dearest blessing possible can come from believing in and experiencing the Holy Spirit.

Henry Drummond, in *The New Evangelism* wrote, "In the New Testament alone the Spirit is referred to nearly three hundred times. And the one word with which He is constantly associated is Power." Jesus promised His disciples, "You shall receive power when the Holy Spirit has come upon you." (Acts 1: 8.)

There has never been anything in all the history of mankind like the spiritual experience of the hundred and twenty persons in the upper room in Jerusalem on the day of Pentecost. Cowered together like frightened sheep, suddenly, "they were all filled with the Holy Spirit" and this filling caused such a commotion that a multitude came together to see what was happening. Peter, three times the denier of Christ, was so completely changed that he preached the first evangelical sermon and converted three thousand souls in one day. This Holy Spirit experience continued and spread. Only a few days later Peter again preached to a multitude and this time converted five thousand men. Soon Phillip went to the half-breed Jews of Samaria and converted large multitudes there. When persecutions arose, instead of the disciples of Jesus becoming weaker, they became stronger. This strength was an entirely different kind of power from any other in the world. This strength was that of being as good and gracious and Christlike as is humanly possible. The only weapons that these people had with which to conquer the world were the love of God and man within their hearts and the words of Jesus on their lips, and the power, guidance, and strength of the Holy Spirit.

No group of people has ever increased with such rapidity and boldness as the first-century Christians. Here is the fifth, and most important reason for believing in the Holy Spirit, and that is that He gives power to ordinary men and women even today to speak God's word with boldness.

Why are the individual Churches and the Universal Church not changing the course of history today in favor of God like the first-century church did? Samuel Shoemaker in his inspiring book, *With the Holy Spirit and With Fire,* wrote, "We lack the breeze of the Spirit to fill our sails, and carry us steadily forward across the angry and uncharted seas of the world." Very, very true, but the average churchmember doesn't even know there is a Spirit that has a breeze to carry anybody anywhere, because this generation is almost ignorant of what the Spirit is and does. The average churchmember feels he must paddle his own canoe, because he does not know that the Holy Spirit is the third person of the Godhead, who not only was the Agent in the Act of creation, incited the prophets and inspired Holy Scripture, overshadowed the Virgin Mary when the atonement was consummated, and filled the members of the first-century church with divine power; but that he is God's life-giving presence in the church today who still gives power, strength, and guidance, directly from the Father and the Son to individuals.

This ignorance on the part of so-called Christians concerning the Holy Spirit has caused imperfect or partial conversions. Jesus said, "I am the way, the truth, and the life." This statement makes Jesus' life the perfect example concerning spiritual things. If, when Jesus came up out of the Jordan after his baptism with water, "The Holy Spirit descended upon Him," why does the Spirit not descend on the new believer today when he is baptized with water? Is it because the new believer has accepted Christ with his mind or intellect and not with his heart or emotions? Was Jesus as good inwardly. (Come unto Me for I am gentle and lowly in heart —Matt. 11: 29) as He acted outwardly? Is this why He both experienced the baptism with water and the Holy Spirit at the same time?

There is one other account in the New Testament of a similar occurrence and that is the experience of the Roman centurion, Cornelius, found in the Tenth chapter of Acts. This soldier and his whole household received the baptism of the Holy Spirit while Peter was still witnessing to them about the risen Lord. This happened even before they had been baptized with water!

Cornelius was a "devout man who feared God with all his household, gave alms liberally to the people, and prayed constantly to God." (Acts. 10: 1.) If a person lived like Cornelius, perhaps he, too, would experience such a blessing—a true conversion with water and the Spirit like Jesus had. If modern Christians do not know and believe in the Holy Spirit, and live in such a way that He can enter into their lives, they will never have a true conversion and carry out God's will for them in this age.

THE PARABLE

OF THE WONDERFUL TEACHER

There was once a Master Musician who came to a certain city to play. Now there was a young boy in that city who went to the concert and heard him perform. As soon as the concert was over, the boy rushed backstage and told the Master Musician that he was the best pianist he had ever heard. The musician thanked him, and explained that the boy could play as well if he would first buy the music of the Great Composer and then study under the Wonderful Teacher.

The boy was filled with delight when he heard the good news that he could play like the Master Musician, and he begged the great master to send him at once to the Wonderful Teacher. The Master Musician smiled, and said, "You will not be able to play as I do, unless you buy the music of the Great Composer. It is his music that I play, because it is the greatest music ever written, and that is why you think it is very beautiful."

The boy went out immediately and bought the music of the Great Composer, and hurried to the home of the Wonderful Teacher. He was happier than he had ever been when he met the teacher and he told the boy he could be a pupil, but only on one condition, and that was, that he must faithfully apply himself to the work and training that the teacher had for him.

"I will do anything you ask," said the boy. "Only let me play like the Master Musician."

At first the lessons were easy and wonderfully interesting to the boy, because the teacher was very kind and understanding, but the Wonderful Teacher was also demanding. Every day, they would go over and over the music of the Great Composer together. Time and time again, they would have to play the passages until they were completely perfect. Occasionally, his hands would fall from the piano, because he was so very tired, but the Wonderful Teacher would lift them gently back upon the keyboard and whisper, "You will never play like the Master Musician until you have the pieces perfectly memorized."

Days turned into weeks, and weeks into months, and the months to years, and the boy still worked away at the music of the Great Composer. Time and again he was disheartened. The piano was often cold and unresponsive under his touch. Occasionally, he missed only a few notes, but the teacher demanded that he play the whole piece over again, and again until there was not one imperfect passage. Finally, they worked together to perfect the smoothness and grace of the music; so that it would be as natural to the boy as it had been for the Master Musician.

These were the hardest times of all, because the boy knew that he could play the music letter perfect, but the teacher coaxed him to perfect even the touch on the keys; so he would become another excellent pupil. At last, the day of his recital arrived, and the boy with nervous hands went to the piano in the great concert hall. There standing in the wings smiling and encouraging him, was the Wonderful Teacher. The boy began to play. How glad he was that he had listened carefully to his good teacher. The beautiful passages of the Great Composer's music flowed from the boy's fingers, and the whole audience strained to listen for each note, because it was so completely perfect. At the end of the last number, the group of eager listeners rose with one accord and applauded for more music. The boy wept for joy, and the Wonderful Teacher came out from the wings and put his arm about the boy and said, "See, you have done just as I told you, and now, you can play like the Master Musician."

LIVING WIND

Living Wind whose sacred breath fills all the earth with
    words divine,
Whisper to us mysteries of Thee.
Hid from the eyes of all, your breezes strangely blow
Upon us mortals here below, thoughts, heavenly.
Living Wind whose aweful power shakes the wicked and the
    proud,
Speak to us humble ones more low,
And guide us through the currents swift.
We do not know which way to go.
Living Wind whose strength sustains the elements, fill our
    drooping sails,
Before we drift into strange water, swift and deep.
Blow us to harbors where our lives will be
Lived in devotion to God's service, sweet;
So we can sail into eternity.

ENTER THE KINGDOM OF HEAVEN
(OR GOD)

When John the Baptist began his ministry, he preached, "Repent ye: for the kingdom of heaven is at hand. (Matt. 3: 2.) After John was cast into prison and Jesus made his home in Capernaum of Galilee, he also preached, "Repent for the Kingdom of heaven is at hand." (Matt. 4: 1.) Again, when Jesus sent out the twelve disciples to try their wings at witnessing (Matt. 10) and when he sent out the seventy and let them do the same thing (Luke 10) he told both groups to announce the Kingdom of Heaven's arrival. Since both John and Jesus began their ministry with these words, and Jesus told his followers to do likewise, a sincere Christian should ask, "What is the Kingdom of Heaven or God?"

Jesus told the Pharisees of his day, "The law and the prophets were until John: since that time the Kingdom of God is preached, and every man presseth into it. (Luke 16: 16) and "The Kingdom of God cometh not with observation: Neither shall they say, lo, here or lo, there! for behold the Kingdom of God is within you." (Luke 17: 20, 21.)

Jesus also told Nicodemus, a ruler of the Jews; "Verily, verily, I say unto you, except a man be born again, he cannot see the Kingdom of God," and "Verily, verily, I say unto you, except a man be born of water and of the Spirit, he cannot enter into the Kingdom of God." (John 3: 3, 5.) From these quotations, the Christian can only draw one conclusion, and that is, a person can enter this kingdom here and now, but this kingdom while on this earth was and is spiritual or heavenly; for Jesus told Pilate, "My kingdom is not of this world." (John 18: 36.)

"Yes," replies the average Christian, "I am convinced there is an earthly Kingdom of Heaven, but why should I enter it?" In the Lord's prayer (better called the disciple's prayer) Jesus said, "Thy kingdom come. Thy will be done, on earth as it is in heaven." (Matt. 6: 10.) A true Christian should want to enter the Kingdom of Heaven in order to do God's will on earth. Here is the first reason for entering the kingdom, and that is that God planned it and wants his children to do so.

Jesus used many parables about property and kingdoms, and in them he always spoke of the inheritance that belonged to the rightful heirs. The most vivid of these is the parable in the Twenty Fifth chapter of Matthew which describes the Last Judgment and he speaks these words to the blessed, "Come, O blessed of my Father, inherit the kingdom prepared for you from the foundation of the world. . . ." Here is the second reason for entering the Kingdom of Heaven, the blessed will receive an inheritance, namely the spiritual gifts. This reason has for many years been almost completely overlooked or so carefully whitwashed that few people know that they have an inheritance awaiting them in the Kingdom. St. Paul in the Twelfth chapter of First Corinthians tells the new Christians that they have received spiritual gifts and they are: Wisdom, Knowledge, Faith, Healing, Miracles, Prophecy, the discerning of spirits, tongues, and the interpretation of tongues. It is the same Spirit today that moved in the first century, and the same gifts are still given, but this generation is so sure that there is nothing of true value that can be known except by the senses that it has completely overlooked this wonderful reason for entering the kingdom.

These spiritual gifts have secular names that really do not

fully explain what they do for a person spiritually, and only in the light of the scripture can these gifts be appreciated. Of these nine gifts, five of them—wisdom, knowledge, faith, prophecy, and the discerning of spirits (or devils) are fairly common to one degree or another in non-Christians. At the time of the "new birth," Baptism of the Holy Spirit, or the entering of the Kingdom of Heaven (and all of these names mean the same thing) some or all of the gifts fill the "True" convert and are at a higher level or more powerful in him than in the ordinary person. These "gifts" do not have a mysterious quality, but the fact that a person completely lacking in one or more of them should suddenly acquire them is a mystery.

It is for this reason that they are seldom mentioned, and the last four are all but completely ignored. There is no getting around the fact that in the spiritual life there are mysteries, and that the last four gifts—miracles, gifts of healing, diverse kinds of tongues, and the interpretation of tongues are such and that they once did and still do exist!

According to Webster's Dictionary, wisdom is the "Ability to judge soundly and deal sagaciously with facts, especially as they relate to life and conduct." If this ordinary ability were suddenly heightened and empowered, a person would suddenly possess the spiritual ability of judging the moral fitness of his or her life as God sees it. It is this gift that turns hardened sinners into saints, and good people into near angels. It was this gift that enabled Jesus to outwit his enemies when they bombarded him with treacherous questions about marriage after death, paying tribute to Caesar, and which was the greatest commandment. For this reason it is considered the greatest gift and James wrote concerning it, "But the wisdom that is from above is first pure, then peaceable, gentle, easy to be entreated, full of mercy and good fruits, without variance."

Knowledge is very different from wisdom in that it is

familiarity gained by actual experience. Learning must take place. Jesus promised his disciples at the Last Supper that when the counselor or Holy Spirit came, he would bring all Jesus' sayings to their remembrance. The priests, and the Sadducees all marveled when "they beheld the boldness of Peter and John, and had perceived that they were unlearned and ignorant men." (Acts 4: 13.) How many people read their Bibles daily and ask for guidance but cannot recall any of it to witness for their Lord! This gift of knowledge is the ability to recall only what spiritual things a person has exposed himself to before or during his new life, and this gift is limited by a person's willingness to study spiritual things, especially Scripture.

This gift of knowledge and Jesus' command to his disciples to go teach, has caused the promotion of education in all places where Jesus is worshipped. Western Civilization did not become what it is because of its superiority, but because it embraced Christianity, and Christ brought truth and learning. The many schools that fill Christian communities are as much a witness to Jesus as the churches.

The gift of faith is a Christian's sorest need. In fact, most Christians sink in the seas of doubt just like Peter, and but for the outstretched hand of the Lord, they would never make it. The gift of faith is the gift of boldness. This gift made the "newborn" Christians of the first century absolutely certain they served a Risen Savior, and this vitalizing certainty sent them into all the world afire with the "good news."

The gift of prophecy is actually the ability to combine wisdom, knowledge, and faith in a peculiar way to interpret events with spiritual meaning. Many "newborn" Christians suddenly become prophets when they see their own children thinking about and playing with nothing but guns and toys of destruction and realize that these children from God will become "sons of the devil" if they are not quickly guided in another direction! Prophecy is the "gift" that enables a person to judge the future by the past according to God's Spiritual Laws, and is a gift every statesman should desire. A nation without leaders who have this gift will fall into desolate days, because if God does not build the house, those who labor, work in vain.

There is actually nothing mysterious about the "gift" of "discerning of spirits." When a person is "born anew" into the Kingdom of Heaven, all things are made new. There is suddenly a longing to communicate in a deeper, more Christ-like way with other people, and as the child of the kingdom forgets himself and watches others more closely, he sees their devils of resentment, lust and fear, for after all, he has experienced these feelings before he was "born anew," and is now able to recognize them in others. In fact, this gift is very common among persons who have experienced a "true conversion" or "new birth."

This age, as no other, has shunned emotionalism in religion, but in nothing else. Hastings, in his *Bible Dictionary*, says that at the time of the baptism of the Holy Spirit when the believer receives spiritual gifts, "the floodgates of emotion are down." Certainly this is a very dangerous experience because, after all, inhibitions disappear temporarily. If it is a genuine experience, it is emotional but only because a person has surrendered his will to the will of God, and this, of course is the dearest blessing possible. Because so many misguided people have only surrendered the control of their emotions to exhibitions of all undesirable kinds, and then declared they experienced the baptism of the Holy Spirit, many, many people shun this experience, especially that of receiving the four last gifts. In fact, the majority of people today believe that these gifts ceased to exist after the first century, and that it is near insanity for a person to believe in them.

Most people considering entering the kingdom think their

experience will be as terrible as that of St. Paul, but the conversion of Jesus and Cornelius and the people of Samaria were all very quiet and gentle and joyous in nature. Jesus himself gave some of the best information about how to have a gentle "new birth" when he said, "And from the days of John the Baptist until now the Kingdom of Heaven suffereth violence, and men of violence take it by force." Only the proud get struck down on the Damascus road.

The many aspects of the gift of miracles would take up a whole book. People still wonder if they should take the miracles of Jesus literally or figuratively. It is obvious that miracles like the feeding of five thousand with only five loaves and a few fishes, the stilling of the angry elements, and the water changing to wine in Cana do not take place today, but thousands of hungry people are fed in the name of Jesus. Mammoth projects to control the elements are built by Christian men, and the putrid waters of indifference to human suffering have changed to sparkling wine of loving concern. Are these not miracles? And are they not carried out by men and women who are filled with the spiritual gift called miracles! Who would ever think of the needs of people whom they have never seen without receiving this "gift of miracles"?

Only the Roman Catholic Church and a few sects believed in the "gift of healing" being present in this age until a few years ago. Leslie Weatherhead in his book *Psychology, Religion and Healing* wrote that most so-called healings in the time of Christ and today were either the psychological use of suggestion on a psychosomatic disorder or else exaggeration on the part of those participating—such as saying Jesus healed lepers when all skin diseases were probably called leprosy, and thus the skin diseases Jesus healed were not true leprosy. If Jesus actually arose from the dead and told his disciples "that these signs shall accompany them that believe . . . they shall lay hands on the sick and they shall recover," (Mark 16: 17-18) it is certain that people still receive the gift of healing even today, and certainly the modern MD is an outstanding example. This being true, then three things are certain:

1. There are persons who receive "gifts of healing."
2. They meet people with faith enough to believe God will heal them—by medication, surgery, and or prayer.
3. The healer then prays and administers to the sick person in the name of Jesus and for the glory of God, and the sick person is healed according to his faith.

This "gift of healing" does not do away with modern medicine. To the contrary, it is the reason for its existence. No infidel or immoral person has ever made any contribution in the science of healing, but only those people of outstanding character have ever left a miracle of healing to posterity. One of the noblest of these people is Mme. Curie, and Albert Einstein in his book, *Out of My Later Years,* has this to say about her: "It was my good fortune to be linked with Mme. Curie through twenty years of sublime and unclouded friendship. . . . Once she had recognized a certain way as the right one, she pursued it without compromise and with extreme tenacity. The greatest scientific deed of her life—proving the existence of radioactive elements and isolating them—owes its accomplishment not merely to bold intuition but to a devotion and tenacity in execution under the most extreme hardships imaginable, such as the history of experimental science has not often witnessed. If but a small part of Mme. Curie's strength of character and devotion were alive in Europe it would face a brighter future."

No, this gift of healing does not do away with modern medicine, because the many hospitals that cover the countryside are as much monuments to Jesus as the churches, because only in Christian countries has medicine kept up with other developments.

There is no doubt that diverse kinds of tongues, and the interpretation of tongues are both scriptural because they appear all through the Acts and New Testament writings other than the Gospels. They have, however, always caused confusion, because the babbling of the new baby to its mother is only understood by the mother and child. St. Paul wrote, "He that speaketh in a tongue edifieth himself, but he that propphesieth edifieth the church . . . I thank God, I speak with tongues more than you all, however in the church I had rather speak five words with my understanding, that I might instruct others also, than ten thousand words in a tongue." (I Corinthians 14: 4, 18-19.) It is always well for a "newborn" Christian to remember that these last two gifts are the least of the gifts and are for private worship only.

As the new member of this kingdom begins to really experience these gifts in his spiritual life—for example a person who is almost always forgetting Scripture suddenly finds he can remember even the most difficult passages—he feels that blessed assurance that he has always read and sung about, and always wondered just what it was. This feeling and the confidence that it brings is the third reason a person should enter the kingdom. It makes a person radiant and confident even in the face of suffering and death, because he knows that there is a God behind this earthly existence who is working out all things to a victorious end, and the member of the kingdom is on the winning team. Even if he is only the water boy, he will share in the glorious feeling of ultimate victory.

This radiance and confidence may seem foolish to the secular world, but to those who have experienced it, it is a bond that not even death can break; and so here is the fourth reason that a person should enter the kingdom, and that is he will enjoy the fellowship or communion of the saints. Why people laugh at this kind of fellowship and love is still a mystery to those who have experienced it. If it were used every day in all the community, it would not be long before all strife and wars would absolutely cease. The acute feelings of loneliness that so many people have would completely disappear, and the kind of fellowship that the disciples shared with Jesus would take its place.

Thomas Carruth in his book, *A Hundred Days of Love*, wrote:

There is no higher treason
Than to do the right thing for the wrong reason.

If the only reasons that a person has for entering the kingdom are for the blessings and fellowship he will receive and enjoy, he is doing the right thing for the wrong reason. The final and fifth reason for a person to enter this kingdom is almost obvious and that is to produce spiritual fruit. When the heavily laden fruit tree drops its fruit into waiting hands, and sometimes upon unsuspecting bypassers, then it has accomplished its purpose in life, and then only. Jesus refused to use his gift of miracles to turn the stones into bread to feed himself, but later he fed over five thousand men in Jewish territory, and four thousand men in gentile territory. He would not jump from the top of the temple to prove his divinity, but he calmed the storm and the fears of his anxious disciples on the Sea of Galilee. He refused the kingship of the world of his day, but he conquered the hearts of men of faith in all the world for generations to come. He produced such magnificent spiritual fruit that men still marvel at its quality and quantity. This last reason is the real reason for wanting to enter the kingdom, and that is to produce the same fruits of the spirit as Jesus.

Jesus did not offer the kingdom to perfect people, for the first beatitude reads, "Blessed are the poor in spirit, for theirs is the Kingdom of Heaven." (Matt. 5: 3.) Immediately the poor in spirit ask, "How shall I enter this kingdom?" Alas, many have tried, but few have succeeded because they do not know that the way is narrow that leads into the Kingdom of Heaven.

The average church member may become alarmed and ask, "I believe Jesus is the Christ, am I not saved?" Yes, anyone who believes Jesus is the Christ, the Son of the Living God, is saved. The thief on the cross was saved, but what a fruitless and wasted life he had lived. Peter was saved; for he confessed Jesus to be the Christ, but still, he betrayed and embarrassed Jesus. On one occasion, Jesus even called him Satan. Are not most so-called Christians just like Peter?—believing in Christ but sometimes acting like devils.

Jesus told his disciples, "Verily, I say unto you, except you be converted and become as little children, you shall not enter the Kingdom of Heaven. Whosoever, therefore, shall humble himself as a little child, the same is greatest in the Kingdom of Heaven." (Matt. 18: 3-4.) Can it be that a Christian must humble himself to be born again before he can enter the Kingdom of Heaven with power? Yes, there is no other interpretation for this passage. But what is humility—especially the humility of a little child? According to Webster's Dictionary, the word humble is synonymous with meek and lowly.

How familiar these words sound to a Christian who had read and heard many times, Jesus' definition of himself, "I am meek and lowly in heart." (Matt. 11: 29.) Is this the humility that allows the new birth? Yes, it must be, because St. Paul also wrote in the 14th chapter of I Corinthians, "But if all prophesy, and an unbeliever or outsider enters, he is convicted by all, he is called to account by all, the secrets of his heart are disclosed; and so, falling on his face, he will worship God."

What is a meek and lowly heart? Better still, just what is the heart? Webster says it is the seat of the affections. One's feelings, if you please. Since the first Commandment reads, "You shall love the Lord your God with all your heart, and with all your soul, and with all your mind, and with all your strength," (Mark 12: 30) it is obvious that Jesus also considered the heart one's feelings and not one's thoughts. This is something most Christians completely ignore; because even the best confessions are about one's thoughts, words, and deeds, and never one's feelings. People have feelings that they never think about, and if there are sins of the heart, most people refuse to believe they are there. Is this why so many people do not see God, because their hearts are not pure? Or do they really not know they have sins of the heart? David wrote in the Nineteenth Psalm, "Who can understand his errors? Cleanse Thou me from secret faults. Let the words of my mouth and the meditation of my heart be acceptable in Thy sight, O, Lord, my strength, and my redeemer." It is probably both.

"The sacrifice acceptable to God is a broken spirit: a broken and contrite heart, O God, Thou will not despise." (Psalm 51: 17.) Every Christian desiring to enter the Kingdom of Heaven with power should make this prayer of David's his own, and then, he should begin to glorify and praise The Lord. The glory of The Lord is a mirror reflecting the wickedness of men, even the "sins of the heart." Then these sins become clearly visible, and there are at least seven of them. Sometimes they are so very terrible and one or more of them so completely control a person's inner life, that they are called devils, and no one is able to cast them out but Jesus. One may humble himself enough to see them and even confess them, but unless he realizes that only through the power of the

Holy Spirit can he be made whole, he will never enter the Kingdom of Heaven with power. These seven sins of the heart are:

I. The "heart sin" or devil of false pride can be called the Little Red Hen Devil. There are always people who can humble themselves enough to see they are not inwardly perfect, but they feel that they can cleanse themselves with enough time and effort. Some of them even feel that it isn't necessary, because everybody has them, and isn't it natural that people have such feelings, and they don't hurt anyone, and so their excuses run on and on, and they never enter the kingdom.

The only thing that cures this heart sin is the gift of Wisdom. The wiser a person is the more he realizes his inadequacy, and therefore, seeks God's help. This was the prayer of Solomon, for wisdom. Humility is not a thing caused by a person's circumstances, but it is a feeling of his own importance, and self-sufficiency, and wisdom is the one sure cure.

II. The second "heart sin" or devil is fear, and this is a fear of spiritual things, and is a direct product of ignorance of Scripture. The devils cried out to Jesus when they recognized him, "What are you going to do with us?" Why do people fear something as wonderful as a spiritual blessing? If people could only begin to see the glories of spiritual things, just catch a wee vision, they would be like the man who sold all that he had for the pearl of great price. "Perfect love casts out all fear," and when people realize God is love, then this heart sin disappears. The spiritual gift that cures this sin is Knowledge, because only by reading the scriptures, can a person fully know the boundless love of God expressed in the life of Jesus.

III. The third "heart sin" or devil is doubt. To think Jesus is the Son of God and believe it in one's heart are two entirely different things. No one will do anything but pray a cool lukewarm prayer about an injustice, unless he feels strongly that there is something wrong. This heart sin causes inactivity and may even lead to spiritual death.

Just as there is a medicine for every physical disease there is a cure for every heart sin, and that cure is the gift of faith. Once a person realizes he doubts in his heart, he should not be frightened of his feelings, because many people have had this heart sin and have overcome it with the gift of faith that the Holy Spirit gives once it has been confessed.

IV. The fourth "heart sin" or devil is that of misunderstanding. Many people think that spiritual truths have a worldly meaning. These people often think the rich are prosperous because they are good; or that a man has good health because he does not sin, etc. Isaiah in the Sixth Chapter tells of these people:

By hearing ye shall hear, and shall in no wise understand;
And seeing ye shall see, and shall in no wise perceive:

For this people's heart is waxed gross,
And their ears are dull of hearing
And their eyes they have closed
Lest haply they should perceive with their eyes,
And hear with their ears,
And understand with their hearts,
And should turn again,
And I should heal them.

These persons completely misunderstand spiritual things, and are forever causing trouble in church and other places by getting all kind of false ideas started. Such persons may even hunt witches. Once again there is a cure.

The gift of prophecy is the one gift that St. Paul highly

recommended, and he did this to keep confusion out of the early church. He felt, and so do all other persons with any common sense, the importance of this gift to both stabilize the individual and the church, because the gift of prophecy gives "insight into the purposes of God so far as these bore upon the existing state of affairs or indicated future developments." (Interpreter's Dictionary page 154.) It is the combining of all the previous gifts with imagination that is divine, and to a person who is forever misunderstanding spiritual truths this is a very real blessing.

V. The fifth "heart sin" or devil is inferiority or guilt. Sometime, somewhere a person has committed a sin or made a drastic mistake or failed miserably in life, and feels deep down in his heart that he is not worthy of the spiritual gifts. According to most studies on alcoholics, this is the basis of their trouble. They feel inferior. Most of them claim they had dominating mothers, but to tell the truth if someone had not run their life for them, they would not have made it.

The startling thing about this heart sin is the cure. The cure is miracles, and at first thought this gift of miracles seems impossible for those who suffer from inferiority and guilt. Moses is the classic Bible example of the man who was possessed with both inferiority and guilt. Having killed a man and then having run away to the back side of nowhere, he was a perfect failure, when God called him with the burning bush experience. Yet, he received the greatest gift of miracles of any of the Old Testament characters with the exception of Elijah. God even saw fit to give him the Ten Commandments.

Why this is true is one of the glorious miracles of God's love, but it is true. One reformed alcoholic was asked by a skeptic, did he believe in miracles? And did he think that the water turned to wine at Cana? The reformed drunk thought a while and said, "Well, I don't know about that, because I wasn't there, but I do know that Jesus turned liquor into food and furniture at my house."

VI. The sixth "heart sin" or devil is that of resentment or hate, and there is not a person who has ever been slighted who has not had to deal with the unholy feeling! Most resentment is well deserved. All along the road of life, people are forever hurting others. Many times this is not intentional, because man is not really wicked, just selfish, and he wants his way or to do things as he thinks they should be done, regardless of the other person's feelings. Children resent their parents' authority, even when it is best for them. Wives resent their many uninteresting and hard chores. Husbands resent their nagging wives. And everyone resents taxes! Resentments held over a long period of time fester into hatred, and the first time the word Satan appeared in the Bible, according to the Bible's Interpreter's Dictionary, this name was literally translated, "to hate." Hatred or Satanic disease can slip up into the inner life and ruin all of life. That is why Christians must forever examine their feelings toward their fellowman, and also toward God.

Sad as it is, it is true that most people hold resentments toward God. It was Eve's resentment of God's control that made her disobey God, and here is where more Christians miss the kingdom than any other place—man cannot reconcile himself to God's control, because he is often ignorant of the fact that most of man's suffering is caused by Satan, and it was Satan's jealousy of God that caused him to entice Eve to disobey God.

It is not God who oppresses man, but Satan. It is the old serpent who caused death and sin and sickness, not the heavenly Father. When Peter witnessed to Cornelius, he said, "Jesus went about . . . healing all that were oppressed by the devil for God was with him." (Acts 10: 38.) Glory be to the

Father who gives us the victory through Jesus Christ, our Lord!

Many people when they realize that they have resentments toward God do not go ahead to beg his forgiveness, but try to run away from what they feel is blasphemy. This is the wrong thing to do, because true blasphemy is a cursing or reviling of God, and resentments are a natural part of human nature. That is why a person should confess these feelings, to become a spiritual person. He has provided the gift of healing for just this purpose, and there is no getting around the fact that man's hate and resentments make him very sick.

This gift of healing is spiritual, of course, and should not be confused with the healing of many physical diseases. That the soul and heart can become sick is even more obvious than the fact of the body and mind being sick. Emotional sickness is by far the hardest to cure, and any person wanting to enter the kingdom should turn himself inside out before God to make sure he rids himself of all resentments and hates; so he can enter the Kingdom of Heaven.

VII. The last or seventh "heart sin" or devil is that of lust or unclean spirits. Jesus was the master artist at recognizing them, and even his presence caused these spirits to speak out. They are in every person who has ever lived, even if they do not cry out loud so others can hear them, because they are a very real part of man's earthly nature. Lusts are the cause of all unclean spirits. There is an old saying, "Your wants will kill you." Yes, O, Yes, one's wants will kill his soul, slowly but surely. Many a person resists most temptations, even in his thoughts, and still "lusts in his heart" or longs passionately for the "things of this world and the deceitfulness of riches." (Matt. 13: 22.)

This is what makes most Christians dissatisfied, cross, and irritable. They are living one way and longing another. They think because they do not want their neighbor's belongings, that they have not broken the commandments, but instead of breaking the last, Thou Shalt Not Covet, they have broken the first. Thou Shalt Love the Lord Thy God With All Thy Heart . . . Ah, no wonder this generation is miserable.

Again the Spirit has the cure—the discerning of Spirits, and when a person knows first aid he can help himself; so he won't be physically ill, and when he can discern spirits, he can quickly hold them up to God, and he will remove them.

The eager Christian asks, "If then, I humble myself and admit I have "heart sins" and confess them to God, realizing that He alone can remove them, will I enter the kingdom?" Yes, and with power. Anyone who does this will be born again and what a change will take place. All the peace and joy that Jesus promised his disciples will be in the "newborn" Christian. How he will glorify God! How he will mourn, not for himself, but for all whom Satan has oppressed. How he will long for righteousness, and oh, how he will read God's word. His Bible will become more interesting than the daily paper; for he must know the word to fight the tempter in the wilderness. Satan will do his best to convince him that this experience did not really happen, but the joy he will find in praying, and the understanding he will now have of the scriptures, and the boldness and power that will fill him and cause his life to be a perpetual witness in his community for Christ, will be all the proof he, or anyone, will ever need to realize he has entered the Kingdom of Heaven with power.

Hallelujah! Salvation and glory and power belong to our God. (Rev. 19: 1.)

THE PARABLE OF THE WISE LADY

There was once a wise lady who had two suitors, who both wanted to marry her. The first suitor was gay and handsome, wore fine clothes, and was always telling her how very much he loved her. The other suitor was not as lighthearted and dashing as the first, but he also told her how very much he loved her. At last, the lady realized that she must make a choice between the two, and choose one of them for a life mate, but she could not decide which one loved her the most, and she was equally attracted to both of them. All her friends encouraged her to choose the first suitor because he was more fun at a party than the second, but she wisely told them that a husband would not be at a party with his wife forever.

The first suitor realized that she was going to choose one of them for a husband; so he brought her a large box of candy and sat down and ate most of it himself, but the second suitor brought her a cook book so that she could read it and soon be a good cook.

It was not long before the first suitor brought her a large rhinestone necklace, and told her to put it on with her evening dress and they could go dancing, but the second suitor gave her a necklace of milk white pearls and told her that he thought they would look pretty on a wedding dress.

Later, the first suitor brought her a large bottle of perfume so she could smell heavenly while she was with him, but the second suitor gave her a setting of fine silver that he told her she could use as a good homemaker forever.

The young lady still did not know just what to do, but she decided to meet the families of the two. She was very disappointed to find that the family of the first suitor was loud and rude, and at times even made fun of her to her face, and she thought, "How miserable I would be in this family." When, however, she went to visit the family of the second suitor, his mother greeted her at the door, and had even prepared her favorite dish for their dinner. Everyone was kind and hospitable to her, and she thought, "How happy I would be in this family."

She went home with her mind almost made up in favor of the second suitor when there was a knock at the door and the first suitor had come to give her one last present. It was a large box with a bright red bow on it, and when she opened it she found it was full of tickets to all the latest shows and passes to the finest clubs. He told her that she could go with him to all these places if they were married. She was greatly impressed and after he left decided that she might marry him after all, but then the second suitor came to call. He handed her a small iron lock box, and told her it was all that he had, but it was hers forever if she would choose him forever, and then he left. When she at last got the box open it was full of paper that she could not understand: so she went to her banker, who always advised her, and asked about them.

The sound banker told her that these papers were the most valuable investments he had ever seen, and that if she took them, she would be increasingly rich and have wealth for herself and her unborn children. When the wise lady realized how very much the second suitor loved her, for he had given her everything that he had, and that it was an investment that would make her and her children rich, she quickly chose the second suitor for her husband.

IMMORTAL LEGACY

Immortal legacy, rejected by the rightful heirs,
Is offered to the orphaned sons of me.
Unworthy and impoverished though we are,
We long for absolution from our sins.
Immortal legacy, containing gifts of wealth unused,
Has been locked up, away from all mankind.
In the tight vault of selfishness and unbelief,
But we have found, humility, the key divine.
Immortal legacy, at last released to us who have searched long
    and hard,
Will surely make us wealthy, wise, and great,
And soon will yield to us, returns whose rate,
Is so fantastic, we can give each friend a share.

PRODUCE SPIRITUAL FRUIT

Many, many people fail to fully understand the purpose of the gifts. At the time of the baptism or "true conversion," there is a cleansing and also a filling. Just as the newborn baby receives presents from his earthly parents; so the spiritual infant receives "gifts" from the Heavenly Father. These are not gifts that are tangible—just as Jesus said in the Fourteenth Chapter of John about the Spirit of truth, "Whom the world cannot receive; for it beholdeth him not," so it is with the spiritual gifts, they are invisible. There is the life within a person and then there is the life outside a person that everyone can see. The spiritual gifts fill the "newborn" and change or convert and equip him for his spiritual growth within, which will produce fruits without that everyone can see. A person must accept the spiritual gifts before he can produce any real spiritual fruit. Jesus warned his disciples and the great multitudes about passing judgment on others, but he realized that sometimes this is necessary; and so he also told them to judge a person's teachings by his fruits.

St. Paul wrote, "Not that I seek for the gift, but I seek for the fruit." (Philippians 4: 17.) The fruits of the spirit are "love, joy, peace, longsuffering, kindness, goodness, faithfulness, meekness, self-control." (Galatians 5: 22.) These words are often rattled off by a person studying the Bible with little thought about their true meaning. The English language is very inadequate when such words as these are translated from the Greek. Dr. William Barclay in his book, *The Letters to the Galatians and Ephesians,* tells the meaning of these words in the original Greek.

"*Love;* the New Testament word for love is agape. This is not a word which classical Greek uses at all commonly. In Greek there are four words for love. (a) Eros means the love of a man for a maid; it is the love which has passion in it. It is never used in the New Testament at all. (b) Philia is the warm love which we feel for our nearest and our dearest; it is a thing of the heart and the feelings of the heart. (c) Storge rather means affection and is specially used of the love of parents and children. (d) Agape the Christian word really means unconquerable benevolence. It means that no matter what a man may do to us by way of insult or injury or humiliation we will never seek anything else but his highest good. It is therefore a feeling of the mind as much as it is of the heart; it concerns the will just as much as it does the emotions. It describes the deliberate effort—which we can only make with the help of God—never to seek anything but the best, even for those seek the worst for us. *Joy;* the Greek word is chara, and the characteristic of this word is that it most often describes that joy which has a basis in religion and whose real foundation is God. It is not the joy that comes from earthly things or cheap triumphs. Still less is it the joy that comes from triumphing over someone else in rivalry or competition. It is a joy whose basis is God. *Peace;* in the contemporary colloquial Greek this word eirene has two interesting usages. It is used of the tranquility and serenity which a country enjoys under the just and beneficent government of a good emperor. And it is used of the good order of a town or a village. Villages had an official who was called the superintendent of the village's eirene; he was the keeper of the public peace. Usually in the New Testament eirene stands for the Hebrew shalom, and means not just freedom from trouble, but rather everything that makes for a man's highest and best good. Here it means that tranquil serenity of heart which comes of the all-pervading consciousness that our times are in the hands of God. It is interesting to note that chara and eirene both became very common Christian names in the Church. *Patience;* Makrothumia; this is a supremely great word. The writer of First Maccabees says that it was by makrothumia that the Romans became masters of the world, and by that he means the Roman persistence which would never make peace with an enemy even in defeat, a kind of conquering patience. Generally speaking, the word is not used of patience in regard to things or events, but of patience in regard to people. Chrysostom said that it is the grace of man who could revenge himself and who does not, of the man who is slow to wrath. The most illuminating thing about it is that it is very commonly used in the New Testament of the attitudes of God and of Jesus towards men. If God had been a man He would have taken His hand and wiped out this world long ago; but God has that patience which bears with all our sinning and which will not cast us off. In our lives, in our attitude to and dealings with our fellow men we must reproduce this loving, forbearing, forgiving, patient attitude of God towards ourselves.

Kindness and *goodness* are very closely connected words. For kindness the word is chrestotes. It, too, is quite commonly translated goodness. But sometimes the Authorized Version translates it kindness and sometimes gentleness. The Rheims Version in II Corinthians 6:6 translates it sweetness. It is a lovely word. Plutarch says that it has a far wider place than justice. Old wine is called chrestos, mellow. Christ's yoke is called chrestos (Matt. 11: 30), that is, it does not chafe and irk and gall. The whole idea of the word is a goodness which is kind. The word which Paul uses for goodness (agathosune) is a peculiarly Bible word and does not occur in secular Greek. It is the widest word for goodness; it is defined as, "virtue equipped at every point." What is the difference? Agathosune might and could rebuke and correct and discipline; chrestotes can only help. Trench says that Jesus showed agathosune when he cleansed the Temple and drove out those who were making it a bazaar; but he showed chrestotes when He was kind to the sinning woman who anointed His feet. The Christian needs that goodness which at one and the same time can be kind and strong. *Fidelity;* this word is common in secular Greek for trustworthiness. It is the characteristic of the man who is reliable. *Gentleness;* praotes is the most untranslatable of words. In the New Testament it has three main meanings. (a) It means submissive to the will of God. (b) It means teachable, the man who is not too proud to learn. (c) most often of all it means considerate. Aristotle defined praotes as the mean between excessive anger and excessive angerlessness, as the quality of the man who is always angry at the right time and never at the wrong time. That which throws most light on its meaning is that the adjective praus is used of an animal who has been tamed and brought under control; and so the word speaks of that self-mastery and self-control which Christ alone can give. Praotes speaks of the spirit which is submissive to God, teachable in all good things, and considerate to its fellow men. *Self-control;* the word is ekgrateia; Plato uses it in the sense of self-mastery. It is the spirit which has mastered its desires and its love of pleasure. It is used of the athlete's discipline of his body, and of the Christian's mastery of sex. Secular Greek uses it of the virtue of an Emperor who never lets his private interests influence the government of his people. It is the virtue which makes a man so much the master of himself that he is fit to be the servant of others."

It is obvious from Dr. Barclay's very detailed interpretation of the Greek meanings of the spiritual fruits, that the average church member is completely ignorant as to their power. In fact, the sin of this generation that will cost more souls than any other is that the only English word that comes close to the agape love of the days of St. Paul, is Charity, and that word was dropped from the Revised Standard Version of the Bible. Now the layman will be completely without an adequate word in English to explain to him that Christian love is willed—and it is good will to all. If all the New Testament writers are correct, this is the most desired fruit, because in the Thirteenth Chapter of 1st Corinthians, is written, "Make love (agape or charity) your aim."

Why does the average church member or Christian not produce large quantities of the spiritual fruit? From the condition of the world, it looks like they should be trying with all sources available to do so, but strangely enough, the spiritual fruits are not mentioned in most sermons today. This may be due to ignorance on the part of the preachers in that they take it for granted that most of their members understand this, but they do not.

Many, many Christians feel that entering the Kingdom of Heaven or experiencing the Baptism of the Holy Spirit is the climax to their spiritual lives. If Jesus is the perfect example, this experience is simply a complete or "true conversion," and is for the life of a Christian what breaking through the dark earth and up to the sunlight is for a plant. It is a short period of pain which leads to the glorious illumination of God's love and is the beginning of the tender plant that later grows and becomes strong enough to produce spiritual fruits.

Jesus said in the parable of the sower that only one out of every four persons who entered the Kingdom of Heaven would bring forth fruit. He even explained to his disciples in the Thirteenth Chapter of Matthew, that the first group will not be fruitful because they do not understand what to do with it, "and Satan will snatch it out of their heart." The second group will even experience the joy of these blessings but not use them because of tribulation or persecution about the word.

The third group will even grow spiritually for some time, but will become so busy and involved in the things and cares of the world that they will even lose the spiritual growth they worked so hard to obtain. Only the fourth group will ever understand what has happened and discipline themselves enough to bring forth fruit a hundredfold.

There is no improving on this warning of Jesus about not being fruitful, but there are some things that a person can do that will keep these things from happening to them, and at the same time bring forth some very real spiritual fruit. The first thing a person can do to produce spiritual fruit is daily Bible reading. Brengel, the famous Salvation Army Captain, in his book *Helps to Holiness,* saw General Booth and told him that he was not converting many souls lately. General Booth replied, "Load and fire! Load and fire!" There is one sure way to produce spiritual fruit and that is for a person to become so familiar with the Bible, that he knows it as well as he knows his own life. Jesus said, "My words are spirit," and anyone who reads even a few verses in the Gospels daily feels a spiritual lift. Knowing the words of Jesus from memory on any given subject—marriage, death, forgiveness, etc., affords a wonderful opportunity for a child of the kingdom to witness for his Lord whenever the occasion arises.

Daily Prayer is another good way to produce spiritual fruit. Prayer is conversation with our Lord and God. Who would think of going even a day without speaking to the people with whom they live! God is the author of all life; everyone should talk to the Father daily. According to the teaching and living of Jesus, prayer should have five parts—glorification of God, confession, thanksgiving, intercession, and petition. Much of the Lord's Prayer is adoration and praise, and this may be why most prayers are so very fruitless—people do not love God with lips of praise. Certainly even fewer people really confess their sins in feelings, thought, words, and deeds. The majority of prayers are so filled with "give me's" that there is no time for "thank you's" and intercession for others. When Jesus blessed the bread and thanked God for it, he fed five thousand with it! He also told Peter that if He (Jesus) had not prayed for him Satan would have sifted him like wheat. If devout Christians were praying for sinners, more souls would be saved!

It is impossible for a child of the kingdom to produce spiritual fruits worthy of the blessings God has bestowed upon him without daily, sincere prayer.

At the Last Supper, Jesus told his disciples, "I am the vine, ye are the branches: He that abideth in Me and I in him the same beareth much fruit; for apart from Me ye can do nothing." (John 15: 5.) Nothing produces spiritual fruit like abiding in the presence of the Lord at all times. If a Christian saturates his thoughts with the life of Jesus (for He is the same yesterday, today, and forever) he can imagine the Lord with him at all times guiding and directing his every feeling and act. Soon this presence or abiding of Jesus gives a Holy expression to everything a person does and it is impossible not to produce spiritual fruit, especially love!

Jesus told His disciples to make their prayers short, but sometimes He went alone for hours or all night, but was it to pray as the average Christian thinks of prayer? Was it to meditate and let God's spirit fill and direct Him to the right decisions and actions? There is very much proof to the fact that Jesus meditated. Here again is an idea about the spirit life that this generation has neglected and that is getting quiet and still and meditating. The people of this age are just too busy for that. In the Twenty Fourth Chapter of Genesis is written, "And Isaac went out to meditate in the field at the eventide: and he lifted up his eyes, and saw, and behold the camels were coming." These camels represented the wealth his father had sent to bring back his new wife and life's mate. Here is another reason children of the kingdom do not produce spiritual fruit in large quantities, and that is, they do not meditate over the wealth of Scripture and prayers that God has sent for them. No one makes an investment without first considering it carefully, and no one should take the rich spiritual gifts of God's kingdom without meditating about their use in his individual life.

After a person considers his gifts and meditates and listens earnestly for God's answers to his prayers, he then must actively carry out God's will in his everyday living. This is an act of the will. Even a child of the kingdom can throw up a barrier here and never produce spiritual fruits. This active campaign of good will or God's will, should always begin in the home. Then, it should spread to the community and finally the world. This will be the most powerful witness a person can hope for, and will win more souls than hundreds of sermons.

Jesus demanded two things of his disciples—utter forgiveness without retaliation, and a constant campaign of loving acts of kindness to everyone whom they met. This means that no one is mistreated or abused in any way by a true Christian, and in all ways possible, the child of the kingdom should be actively doing good for others.

Jesus also made one other demand of his disciples when He said, "every branch that beareth fruit, he cleanseth it, that it may bear more fruit." (John 15:2.) Perhaps this is why most Christians do not produce fruit a hundredfold, because they are not willing to be pruned! Almost every fruit-bearing Christian, sooner or later acquires too much foliage and too little fruit. This cutting away of the excess by God always involves suffering on the part of the Christian, and for this reason, any child of the kingdom desiring to produce large quantities of spiritual fruit, should pray that God will cleanse any excess of selfishness or self glory seeking and prune the full-grown vine so that it will yield fruit a hundredfold!

This state of fruit-bearing that some people reach in their own lifetime is truly "Heaven on Earth." It is of itself its own reward, especially the abiding with Jesus in the here and now. That state of Paradise which Jesus promised to the thief on the cross is already here. Death holds no fear, no, not even a sting, because then a child of the kingdom knows that Milton's words in *Paradise Lost* are really true:

"What if earth
Be but the shadow of heaven, and things therein
Each to the other like, more than on earth is thought?"

This makes all accidents, disasters, and worldly woes as scratches on the hand of one who is cutting a rose. Even the experience of death itself seems like an unfamiliar door that will open upon a dearer and more familiar scene than the present one.

THE PARABLE OF THE OASIS GARDEN

There was once a dry and barren land, and the only bright spot in it was the oasis where the River of Life flowed. All the rest of the earth was parched and sterile; so that no fruit grew in the land that could be eaten, except in the oasis. Now the king's son kept the garden and cared for all the fruit trees, and every year he sent out the counselor for the king to travel up and down the land distributing books and making speeches inviting the people to come and learn how to garden in the oasis.

After the counselor had gone out, many people would come to the oasis and ask the king's son to teach them to grow the beautiful trees with edible fruit on them, and each time, this would happen.

First the king's son would ask the prospective gardeners to completely give themselves into his service, forsaking all else. At least half of the applicants would turn away. Then to the remaining group, he would offer the tools that they were to use. First there was the heavy book that they must read full of instructions; then there were the many garden tools that were heavy and often cumbersome that they must bring to work each day as they followed the king's son about the garden as he worked with the soil and the plants. Then there were hours and hours of hard labor that they must do to prepare the soil before the plants were to germinate, and many more quit when they saw what learning to garden like the king's son involved.

Of the little group that remained, about a fourth quit, because they could not understand the book, and carry the heavy tools, and follow the many instructions they received, but the rest of the group kept right on working to produce the full-grown tree, which would have some edible fruit.

It was not many days, however, until those who had quit came back to the garden and stood close to where the faithful ones were working, and began to make fun and throw stones at the gardeners. This was because they were really jealous deep down inside, because they could not keep up with the faithful gardeners, but many of the group did not know this, and so they quit too. Now only half of the group that decided to learn how to grow the fruit trees were still working for the king's son.

It was not long before the plants began to grow and shoot up tall, and the gardeners were very happy because they knew it would not be long before the plants would produce fruit, but half of the remaining gardeners began to remember their many duties at home, and the fun that they had had when they were not working, and they were not being paid with the same wages as they had been before they joined the king's services, and so little by little, they wandered away. The king's son was very discouraged because only three faithful gardeners remained, and he turned to them and said, "Are you going to leave me also? When this fruit comes in, you will have more than all the others in the land."

"No," replied the three faithful gardeners, "We are going to learn to produce fruit like you." And they followed him and his instructions as best they could. It must be admitted, however, that they were all of different dispositions and talents. And the first faithful gardener was a little lazy and scatterbrained; and so he did not water his plants regularly, and quite often did not stop to consider his teacher's orders carefully. When his fruit came in, it was not quite perfect, but the king's son accepted it anyway, because he had been faithful. Now the second faithful gardener longed to have the tallest tree; and so he did not prune his tree. This made the tree so tall that the fruit grew only in the very top of the tree, and he soon found that he and anyone else had great difficulty in gathering his scant crop, but it was good fruit, and the king's son accepted it.

Finally, the third gardener saw how things were going, and so he listened carefully to what the king's son told him. Faithfully, day after day, he watered his plant and tended it, and when he saw that it was growing too tall and turning to nothing but limbs, he quickly cut it back to the right size. When at last his tree had its fruit, it was perfect, and so close to the ground that even the little children passing by could reach up and gather some. Moreover, his tree was so laden with fruit that the king's son came and told him, "This is the kind and amount of fruit my Father always longed for us to have."

Now when the king came to inspect his oasis garden, he too was pleased that at least three gardeners had been faithful, and he allowed them to stay in his garden forever.

SEED OF HEAVEN

Seed of Heaven, planted in each human heart,
Germinate and grow into a plant divine.
Accept the spirit rains on your hard coat.
Burst and push a stem up to the sacred sunshine.
Seed of Heaven, hidden from the eyes of all the world,
Push down into the cold, dark earth a large tap root,
to anchor you against the winds of discontent;
Then raise above the earth a bright green shoot.
Seed of Heaven, stretch yourself, and spread out limbs with
    leaves.
Enlarge yourself, and raise your trunk toward heaven above.
Bloom and mature. Accept the pruning knife;
So you may yield much perfect fruit of love,
And prove to all, you are the Tree of Life.

JESUS AND PRAYER

June Wood — 1962

Prayer is conversation with God, and for this reason many people are afraid to pray. First, because they do not know God, and also because they do not know what to say. At the Last Supper, Jesus told His disciples, "He who has seen Me has seen the Father." Knowing Jesus is knowing God, and it is easy for a person to converse with someone he knows. Even the slightest acquaintance with Jesus, as revealed in the Gospels, assures a person that God is lovingly concerned and anxious to commune with His children.

Jesus also said, "I am the way, the truth, and the life." (John 14:6.) This means He is the supreme authority on all spiritual matters, including prayer, and his sayings reveal many hidden treasures that will help anyone who is longing for a fruitful prayer life.

Many people wonder where, when and in what position to pray. Jesus stressed again and again that it was important to pray in secret. He even went so far as to say: "When you pray go into your room and shut the door and pray to your Father who is in secret." (Matthew 6:6.) The Gospels record that He often went apart or alone to pray, and before He chose the twelve disciples He prayed alone on a mountain all night! He recommended that if people prayed together, it should be in small groups—two or three. This was for the sake of agreement, because where two agree together in prayer and pray in the name of Jesus, He will be present. It is almost impossible to have agreement in prayer with a large group. The 120 in the upper room on Pentecost is the rare exception for they were all together in one place and of "one accord."

When Our Lord drove out the money changers from the temple He said, "It is written, 'My house shall be called the house of prayer'; but you have made it a den of thieves." He also told His disciples in the parable of the publican and the Pharisee that both men went into the temple to pray. From these two statements, a Christian can only conclude that one should also pray in church and this should be a very high form of worship.

Jesus, however, did not put any limit on where or when to pray. Quite often He would break into prayer while He was teaching His disciples, and He even told the woman at the well of Samaria that the day was coming and now is when people would not go to Jerusalem to worship but would worship God everywhere. He also told the parable of the importunate widow to His disciples "to the effect that they ought always to pray and not lose heart." (Luke 18:1.)

The position for prayer was never mentioned by Jesus. He did say that those who prayed in public places or the temple would stand, but He did not recommend this position any more than any other. In fact, in the garden of Gethsemane, Jesus according to Luke, knelt down to pray, while Matthew wrote that he went a little further and fell on his face and prayed.

Actually, Jesus was more concerned with the prayer's attitude or "feelings" than with his position. He even went so far as to tell the Pharisees, "You hypocrites! Well did Isaiah prophesy of you, when He said:

"This people honors me with their lips,
but their heart is far from me."

Our Lord commended the tax collector who stood afar off, with bowed head, and prayed, "God be merciful to me a sinner," and declared he would be justified because, "everyone who humbles himself will be exalted."

No feeling or attitude is as needed on the part of the prayer as faith. When the disciples marveled that the fig tree Jesus had cursed withered in a day, He told them, "Whatever you ask in prayer, you will receive, if you have faith." When the Syro-Phenician woman begged Jesus three times to heal her daughter, Jesus told her, "O woman, great is your faith, be it done for you as you desire." Most people believe that God hears and answers prayers for other people, but they wonder if He would for them. Jesus again and again assured the multitudes that they should have faith in God to care for each one personally. He even said, "Consider the lilies of the field how they grow, they neither toil nor spin, yet I tell you, even Solomon in all his glory was not arrayed like one of these. But if God so clothes the grass of the field, which today is alive and tomorrow is thrown into the oven, will He not much more clothe you, O men of little faith?"

The very fact that Jesus called God, Father, and told others to do so, reveals that He felt God was interested in each person as a Father is interested in each child.

He first instructed His followers to pray the Lord's Prayer in the Sermon on the Mount. Later when He was praying, one of His disciples said to Him, "Lord, teach us to pray." Again He gave the *Lord's Prayer*. This prayer has three definite parts of which Adoration and Praise is the first and most important part. Perhaps this is one reason that most prayers do not get better results, they are not praising the Lord nor seeking His will. Anyone, beginning to pray, should read through the Bible to find suitable words of praise. The Book of Psalms has many beautiful songs of praise. The 103 and 150 Psalms are but two examples. The Book of Revelation, however, has even more beautiful praise, because Jesus is also adored. In the Fifth and Seventh Chapters of Revelations are found the most beautiful and perfect praise in the Bible.

The Lord's prayer also has petitions in it—first for daily bread, and then for deliverance from temptation and evil. Jesus told His disciples immediately after He had given them the Lord's Prayer that, "everyone who asks receives. . . . If you, then who are evil know how to give good gifts to your children, how much more will the Heavenly Father give the Holy Spirit or (good gifts) to those who ask Him?" The gifts of the spirit are wisdom, knowledge, faith, prophecy, gifts of healing, miracles, discerning of spirits, diverse kinds of tongues, and the interpretation of tongues. (I Corinthians 12:8-10.) The greatest of all spiritual gifts however, is grace or divine love which St. Paul so beautifully explains in the Fifth Chapter of Romans. To grow in grace (or divine love) should be a prayer's most earnest petition.

When Jesus saw the large crowds that followed Him, He turned to His disciples and told them to pray for laborers in God's harvest. Any person seeking to do God's will should pray for laborers while he is asking for things from his Father.

Confession is a very important part of the Lord's Prayer. The words "forgive us our debts, as we also have forgiven our debtors," leaves the prayer with one sure way to forgiveness, and that is to forgive. One should, therefore, consider all his offenders first and love his enemies, and pray for all those who persecute him, before he asks for forgiveness. Since our Lord declared that to Love God with all one's heart, soul, mind, and strength, was the first commandment, a person should confess any feelings, thoughts, words, or deeds, that would displease God, and because it is almost impossible for anyone to see his own heart sins, a person should at this time pray the prayer of David: "Clear Thou me from hidden faults."

Since most sins are those of omission instead of commission, a person's confessions should include all his neglects of spiritual things—good deeds, prayer, Bible reading, etc.

The Lord's Prayer did not include thanksgiving and intercession. Jesus, however, used these types of prayers during His ministry. He fed the multitudes on two occasions with only a few loaves and a few fish, after he had given thanks, blessed, and broken the bread. This is probably why most Christians do not receive abundantly anything they want, because they have not thanked God for what they already have. A Christian's greatest blessing is Jesus, and every prayer of thanksgiving should begin with, "Thank you God for Jesus."

At the Last Supper, Jesus told Peter, "but for My prayers, Satan would have sifted you like wheat." After the transfiguration, when Jesus came down from the mountain and found His disciples could not heal the epileptic boy, He told them, "this kind never comes out except by prayer and fasting." These statements clearly show Jesus prayed almost constantly for others—mostly the sick, sinful and sorrowing, and expects his follower to also pray for others.

According to the words and deeds of Jesus there are five parts to prayer: Praise, Confession, Thanksgiving, Intercession, and Petition. Anyone who earnestly prays according to these teachings of Jesus every day, will find that they will soon feel a constant abiding of His presence which will satisfy their spiritual hunger and direct them to higher, more Christ-like living.